GRÈS

© 2004 Assouline Publishing for the present edition
601 West 26th Street, 18th floor
New York, NY 10001, USA
Tel.: 212 989-6810   Fax: 212 647-0005
www.assouline.com

Translated from French by Uniontrad

Color separation: Gravor (Switzerland)
Printed by Grafiche Milani (Italy)

ISBN: 2 84323 416 6

GRÈS

LAURENCE BENAIM

ASSOULINE

t hey called her *"The Great Grès," "The designer's designer," "L'éminence Grès."* "I have nothing to say and everything to show. All I do is work, work, work. When I'm not sleeping, I'm cutting. That's my life." The only peers that this turbaned enigma admired were Cristobal Balenciaga and Yves Saint Laurent. She was ultra-secretive, her neck forever hidden beneath a white cotton scarf or one of her beige-cashmere, turtleneck sweaters. "For the inauguration of the *Belle Époque*, we greatly admired that long blue taffeta coat made by Alix, with the sleeves completely covered with flower petals..." the elegant women of the Golden Age whispered to each other. She dressed La Begum, Grace Kelly and Jacqueline Kennedy. She preferred to present herself through the attire in which she dressed celebrities for single nights, choosing to revel in some distant ball from the quiet of her workshop.

For each collection, she claimed she "completely" wore out three pairs of scissors. She liked to define herself as a "home-worker." Long after her death, her virtuosity continued to intrigue fashion designers: "Her dresses are so incredibly fine. Where did she hide so many yards of fabric?" wondered a fascinated Alber Elbaz. Alix Grès was the absolute paradox of her profession; her ephemeral imprint conceals the riddle of her style within yards of jersey. "I give the dress I create the line and shape that the fabric itself seeks," she would say, hovering like a shadow at the foot of her twisted, draped creations.

She liked artificial silk in indefinable gray-blues, "off-whites," and "the colors of Crete and its light". She designed for women who were slim as Tanagras and turned ivory into the new black. A revolutionary, she was one of the first designers to use "new fabrics," as they called them in the early '30s, and to display shorts in high-fashion shows. Resembling a young mother, she seemed superior with inspired eroticism. The American press quickly described her as someone who enjoyed "dogs [and] walking," who rarely went out and who had "a reputation for being indifferent to what other designers are doing[1]."

first, she wanted to be a sculptor, then a ballerina. She dreamed of sewing without thimbles or needles. Born in 1903, she started out as a woman's hat maker. Next, she set up shop in a three-room apartment on Paris's Rue Miromesnil. Under the name Alix Barton, she sold her dress prototypes, or "fabrics", to commission merchants who exported them in Europe and to the United States. In 1934, she was hired as a dress designer by a company on Faubourg Saint-Honoré that was opened by one of her friends. Her earliest identifiable designs are for sports clothes (a tennis outfit drawn in *Vogue* in June 1933) and street clothes (seamless coats). However, it was as a virtuoso of *Parthenon* draperies that this enemy of social events made her mark, the spirit of which Lucien François described as: "Respect for femininity, strict architecture of lines, difficult economy of means, dignified attitudes, and paradoxically, the instinct of desire[2]."

She was the first to use silk jersey, woven specially for her: "Djersafyn, Derjsyl, Dersatimmix, etc. To counter the graphic bareness of the

1920s, she employed the waves and volutes of skin-skimming fabrics. Her designs – famous in the wake of the decorative arts and architecture of the 1930s – instigated the comeback of the frieze and the arabesque. They enhanced illusion through an art, emphasized in a unique manner, that recalled the "back to basics" and "traditional know-how" approach. While Madeleine Vionnet's bias emphasizes the figure, Grès's draperies are a tribute to movement through careful utilization of the fabric whose "soul and personality" she claimed she could recognize with a mere touch.

as Alix, she experienced her first successes designing costumes for Jean Giraudoux's play *La guerre de Troie n'aura pas lieu*, directed by Louis Jouvet and produced in November of 1935 at the Théâtre de l'Athénée in Paris. "Madame Alix made a point of not dressing up the living that have just been born like resuscitated corpses," wrote Jean-Louis Vaudoyer. She dressed Léda in a white and gold dress, she made the tunic of Priam's wife out of "beetle and forget-me-not colored" pleats and shrouded Peace in snowy veils. Although she painstakingly maintained a low profile, this somewhat Ionian and perhaps Spartan Parisian put on all her finery. "Past and present combine opportunely, tonight, through almost secret exchanges, delicate reconciliations, subtle compensations…"

In the time immediately before World War II, the stars of the world and the stage flocked to this new "star of elegance." Her royal clients included the Duchess of Talleyrand, the Countess Munose, Princess Matilda of Greece, Lady Deterling, Lady Mendl, the Duchess of Windsor and the Princesses of Bourbon-Parma. She dressed Marlene Dietrich at her peak and Argentina in her twilight.

6

Even gems such as Greta Garbo, Vivian Leigh, Dolores del Rio, Yvonne Printemps, Arletty, Sylvana Mangano and Madeleine Renaud were in her golden book. Her complicated draperies attracted the most eccentric clients: one even ordered the same design six times. Christian Bérard claimed that Alix "had overcome gravity." Among her first muses was Isadora Duncan, the first dancer to dance barefoot in a short tunic.

The *"Hellène de Paris"* was to continue her odyssey. She created stage costumes for *Le Voyage de Thésée* (Geroges Neveux, 1943), *La Cantate de Narcisse* (Paul Valéry, 1945), *Amphytrion 38* (Jean Giraudoux, 1947 revival) and *Antigone* (Jean Anouilh, 1952 revival). Her designs were also requested for the tours of *Phèdre* and *Britannicus*, and for Kirk Douglas' *Hollywood rendition of Ulysses* (1953).

a proponent of the French neoclassic style, she seemed to have found unlimited inspiration from distant lands, perhaps revealing a call from far away. Stylistic influences from Chinese pagodas to Japanese *origamis*, and from saris to icon archangels were evident throughout her work. "Did Alix find the inspiration for this suit in Tibet?" *Vogue* wondered about a colt hide coat photographed by Horst. Her answer was another question: "It's strange, this attraction I have for the Far East. Where could it come from?" From burnoose-coats (1934) to Egyptian-style slip-ons (1937) to seamless cotton duck poncho-dresses for the beach (1972), she incorporated the techniques of people from nowhere to sprinkle the Parisian skies with her cosmopolitan stars. Paris, the capital of a boundless universe for which the whole world envied and loved her. "How do the models fasten the dresses, and how to do they get out of them?" wondered *Women's Wear Daily.*

There seemed to be no end to this puzzle. Take, for example, Madame Grès's *manche-kimono:* a design without armholes that follows the natural line of the shoulders, dramatically offsetting the ordinary, ample and free effect. A plain flip-flop with gold-colored leather lacing could replace any high-heeled shoe in the world. In 1935, she transformed shantung summer slacks into a serul. American women loved her famous "pool robes". These high-fashion djellabas matched perfectly with butterfly-frame eyeglasses and a dry martini, while one lounged by a turquoise pool.

I n 1937, she presented her work at the *Exposition Universelle* in Paris and won first prize in Haute Couture. Due to disagreements with her associates, she left the firm and opened her own company in 1942, called Grès. The name was an anagram of her husband's first name: Serge Czerefkov. Shortly after she married the Russian painter in 1937, he left France for French Polynesia – and forgot to return. In her solitude, she was consumed by the intensity of her love for the fabrics that tempted her creator's imagination. Even the barking of her faithful Pekinese, Musig, barely interrupted her musings.

"You have to want to make something with something. These draped dresses, people say it's from Antiquity. But I was never inspired by Antiquity. Before this fabric [a very fine silk jersey] existed, I never thought of making draped dresses. But as soon as I had the fabric, it fell into place by itself. The Greek sculptors made their sculptures using fabrics that lent themselves to their work[3]."

Despite her proclaimed detachment, she seems to have mixed her blood with that of Ictinos and Callicrates, architects of the famous Parthenon and masters of order and proportion. "For me, working fabric or stone is the same thing."

Silk jersey was her marble and women's bodies her living pillars. Her extraordinary hands concentrated on working in the way one shapes an architrave, a frieze or a cornice, carving the fabrics. The strict flutes blend into graceful volutes. Thus, from Athena's temple, her heroines surged, teasing the caryatids of Erechtheus's podium, carrying baskets filled each night by the divine winds. Like the slender columns, her designs offer themselves with the suppleness of curves tamed by lines. The same, omniscient eye that searched, removed and lightened could also dress the modern-day Diana in a plain, linen fabric tennis dress, and clothe the Greek sailors on stage with garnet-red sweaters. Her *Temple au Paradis* dress, dated 1936, revealed her attraction for a past that she was able to render immediately modern with a quick cut of the scissors.

In 1939, she was not afraid to create an Antiquity-style bas-relief to exhibit one of her *Vogue*-celebrated draperies in the High Fashion Room in New York. The masterpieces of Lanvin, Worth, Jean Patou, Paquin, Molyneux, Schiaparelli and others were also displayed. "We gave more importance to the presence of Alix, draped in Djersafyn, a very fine wool jersey by Rodier, because we felt that she had perfectly synthesized the goal we had set for ourselves," explained the magazine in June 1939. There stood this ideal female figure, a stone silhouette grazed by a light fabric that brought it back to life, moving it, like a wave breaking gently over rocks. Only in Madame Grès was the mystery incarnated of a firm, gentle hand that shaped and caressed, twisted without "puckering," wound without straining, bared while dressing her "statues in the flesh" with slip-ons so intricate that one can barely understand just where they start and where they end.

Edmonde Charles-Roux once characterized her as "a dictator disguised as a mouse[4]." Embracing fashion design the way others take their religious vows, she became "Madame Grès," famous and unconventional in her lifetime, a small, fragile-looking woman, an "angry timid woman", with a gentle voice dissimulating an iron temperament. "She has something tense and intense about her that immediately surprised me," recalls a witness. Célia Bertin described her as: "Small, thin, dressed in a gray wool dress and a buff sweater, her sleeves slightly pulled up on her thin arms, she looked like a Sunday school monitor[5]."

a t 1 rue de la Paix, her fashion store was as austere as a boarding school with mirrors: no accessory shop, no ornaments, cream-colored walls, light-colored wood furniture and wall-to-wall carpet. "Her secretive nature is such that you require more cunning to get her to admit who she is than to extort a secret from a Mafia boss," claimed Edmonde Charles-Roux. Lucien François perceived her in much the same way: "silent, but watchful". "She controls everything. Fragile in appearance only, she is driven by fierce energy. A fine face with a broad forehead forever shrouded in a turban, and eyes which despite herself always sparkle with mischief, such is Madame Grès[6]."

She hid everything. Her dresses seem to declare one of her favorite expressions: "Be quiet." She never disclosed her exact birth date, never handed out her passport, even when she traveled in a group. While Chanel exaggerated about how poor her family was, Grès exaggerated about her family riches. She claimed to come from a family of industrialists when in fact she grew up in the modest *petit bourgeois* town of Sucy-en-Brie, in the Val-de-Marne.

During the German occupation, Madame Grès again sewed confusion: legend has it that, six months after it opened, her fashion company was closed in 1942 by the Germans for having displayed blue, white and red evening gowns. Others claim she was closed down because she used fabrics that were obviously purchased on the black market: Madame Grès refused to follow the restrictions imposed on the use of fabrics. She tended to order her artificial silk knitwear and her jerseys directly from manufacturers, and in large quantities. Seeking refuge in the Pyrenees during the war, she returned to Paris when it was liberated, wearing the angora jersey turban that was to become her hallmark.

When her company reopened in 1945, she continued to work according to rules that were eventually considered anachronistic, though her dresses were popular for their modernity. While the 1950s were the time to experiment with lines and volumes, Madame Grès used her materials – from which she was able to extract their infinite reflections – to pay tribute to female body. She maintained a more intimate relationship with that body, whose lines reveal fluidity and dynamism: Madame Grès took Helanca nylon, used for bathing suits, wove it with Lurex, and created an evening gown.

"They created wonderful fabrics for me," Madame Grès would often say. The Bianchini firm created a fabric exclusively for her: silk and metal lamé with Persian motifs. A total of 26 meters were woven at a rate of seven centimeters per day! That was in 1938, and many people sensed a return to "the luxurious habits of old."

In 1950 she created a new line of chic summer outfits. Their immaculate, mid-length and slightly slashed cotton skirts made her and Claire Mac Cardell pioneers in *sportswear*. On her magic carpet, Madame Grès continued to travel around the world. In 1959, she won acclaim for her *Himalaya* coat that was made using web sewn with twine, the ampleness of which begins under the arms. Her long-panel dresses grazed the waist, evoking the *kangra* worn by Punjabi women. Without realizing that she was designing in the beatnik style, she presented shepherd's coats in high fashion shows, was the first to use reversible fabrics and was one of the pioneers of the shift "to fit everyone."

*a**uvent* sleeves, hooded dresses, overcoats using *clam* shapes, oval or spiral-veiled slip-ons, *coulante* dresses, diagonally-wound bodices: technique became an all-consuming quest, an objective pushed to its most extreme. In a church-like atmosphere, she created suits "whose black reminds one of a country parish priest," and launched the *pince-ogive*. "She's the fairy Melusina attempting to pass herself off as a nun, she's an abbess driving a Mercedes," stated Edmonde Charles-Roux. In 1968, Charles-Roux assumed that the painting by Ingres hanging in his living room, *Le Jugement de Béatrice Cenci,* was the reason behind Madame's ever-present turban. In her fashion company she had absolute authority. Rejecting all advice, she finally gave way, like many creative people, to the flattering remarks of a small following.

Unlike Dior, who developed a license agreement policy as early as 1948, Madame Grès refused to put her name on any models other than high-fashion dresses. Their meticulous execution, millimeter fold by millimeter fold – up to 300 hours of work – increased the company's deficit. Some clients were actually dressed for life – free of charge. In 1959, she finally agreed to put her label on a perfume, calling it *Cabochard* – a colloquial term that refers to very stubborn people. This Cyprus, ambergris, fruity, woody, spicy fragrance in a bottle with the famous black velvet bow, sold around the world. Others were to follow – from *Grès pour homme* (1965) to *Quiproquo* (1976) – but *Cabochard* remained the most popular.

It's no fun, but you have to", she said about ready-made clothing. "This profession is about throwing art into business[7]." In 1980, she finally agreed to launch a ready-made clothing line that included scarves and later neckties. The designer Peggy Huyn Kinh, who was hired to create the ready-made models, still has detailed memories of this Parisian cloister. Madame guarded it closely: she always kept the firm's keys attached to a belt around her waist. "She had a 'female Bluebeard' side to her. Chilly beneath her fox-fur lined coats. Gentle and protective with the people she liked, curt with everyone else. Jealous in friendship. One day, I wasn't able to see her. She was offended. I was never to see her again…" The first attempt at the ready-made clothing business lasted just two seasons. The decline had started.

In 1982, Madame Grès was forced to sell the perfume business, her most profitable venture. She reinvested the money in her haute couture company, but in 1984 she finally sold it to Bernard Tapie, a businessman close to François Mitterrand. At that time, he was thought to be an aggressive, young entrepreneur whose reputation had not yet been soiled by lawsuits and scandals. Nevertheless, she refused to give up one ounce of her power, never relinquishing her full authority despite her 80 years. "I, Sir, am in museums, and you will never be!" she is said to have told Bernard Tapie in a fit of rage. Out of respect for Madame Grès, the workers refused to develop the ready-made prototypes whose new launch was announced. There were reports in the press that Bernard Tapie planned on launching "a line of office furniture" under the Grès name. The workshops stood behind Madame Grès; it was a matter of loyalty. She was always extremely generous with her long-term personnel, offering one chief dressmaker a gold bracelet, settling the burial expenses for the husband of another and being called "Mamouschka" by Muni, her protégé. Marc Audibet, who created two collections of ready-made clothing for Grès in 1984, at the request of the Tapie Group, remembers: "There was no organization – she used irons from the 1930s – and she had no respect for ready-made clothing. The only thing she cared about was haute couture. The dresses were her life. This passion of hers was unique, grandiose."

"My only wish was to impress with dresses that were meant to impress the world." She did not drink, smoke, or go out, but said she was "very interested in the punks" she met one day in a television studio: "They were what they were, taking the wrong path, but very proper and very genuine[8]." Her ability to dissimulate herself protected her better than a bulletproof vest.

It is hard to imagine this character, with her austere appearance and birdlike appetite, who liked Haute Époque furniture, XVIIth century Dutch paintings, Byzantine crosses, luxury cars and white roses. Madame Grès was not afraid to go to the flea market with a torn raincoat, traveling by chauffeured Daimler. She had the seats of her navy blue Jaguar covered with mink. She had her car equipped with a television she never watched. "She arrived at her Rue de la

Paix store with her bundle of fabrics," remembers Jeanine Caville, a former chief dressmaker, not without emotion. Leaving the designs to her sewing experts, Madame Grès preferred to cut and pin the fabric herself on the wood dress forms. "We basted, we adjusted the models on the young girls. Then the real work began. We draped, pleat by pleat, always with round needles. We presented the models to her. We stood in line, silently, in front of the studio. She was very impressive, less towards the end, though."

With her scissors hanging from a ribbon like a crucifix, she changed her name the way others change dresses. Germaine Emilie Krebs. Marcelle Alix. Alix. Alix Grès. Alix Barton. In her company that was located in the heart of the building used as the set for the Jules Dassin film *Du rififi chez les hommes* (1954), she mopped up the debts of those close to her – she paid her entire life, afraid of being caught guilty. In 1974, for failing to execute a contract, she was ordered to pay 10 million francs to her American dealer, Mr. Stern. She paid "*in cash, as the happy beneficiary would say,*" she stated with an ironic tinge in an editorial addressed that year to Jacques Fauvet, then the director of the daily *Le Monde*.

A mystery hovers over this woman, who some say "was pushed out of the picture by her daughter Anne," "the one who had her buy a river barge and so many other things." Others say she was ruined. Yet others say she was mad. In the 1980s, when shoulders were getting wider on the fashion podiums, and artificial corsets were used to create unnatural bodies, Madame Grès continued to present her naiads in discreet pearl-gray parlors. Tradition had it that her fashion show was the last one of the season. Among her faithful clients were Princess Gersande de Sabran, daughter-in-law of the alleged King of France, and the Baroness de Rothschild. Issey Miyake was one of her great admirers. Because they represented the quintessence of classical taste, the Venuses and Dianas of Madame Grès never seemed to fail. "You cannot undress a woman. You must respect her; nudity is indecent. A sweater should not cling to her body, hair should be normal, done up properly[9]...." She had a tendency to sermonize that did not alter her premier vocation – to be daring – which Gérard Lefort pointed out in 1984 in the daily *Libération:* "Riff-raff cuts and libidinal openings confirm that the highly honorable Madame Grès still remains the most marvelous brash little girl[10]."

Y et her dresses vanished, like goddesses sucked up by misfortune, sold, scattered like her archives, whose cruel absence is definitely a blot on the beautiful world of fashion. This same cruel world let the great woman witness the liquidation of her company in 1987, during her own lifetime. Three stories emptied in one day. A shattered life. "They broke the furniture and the wood dress forms with axes. The fabrics and dresses were taken away in garbage bags. The place was completely sacked," Anne Grès told me. "No one said a word. I had forbidden Julio, the chauffeur, to drive my mother there. She came. I can still see her in her little black dress. She looked like a ghost. On that day, she realized that her life had been stolen away[11]."
In 1990, Anne Grès left Paris with her mother and her son and went to Saint-Paul-de-Vence (Alpes-Maritimes), where the family owned a housing development along the east ramparts. A year later,

Madame Grès was put in an Alpes-Maritimes retirement home for 335 francs a day. The home was specialized in old-age mental pathologies. In August 1993, she was put in another home where she died three months later. Her death was not announced. With its disclosure in *Le Monde*, on December 14th, 1994, Anne finally agreed to talk: "First of all, I wanted to protect her. All these people who took advantage of her would have found a way to shine again at her expense […]. It's a love secret."

On the collection program, she was still listed as the honorary president of the *Chambre Syndicale de la Couture* of Paris. She even sent out invitations for the traditional season cocktail party… All this was done, even after Madame Grès had been dead for one year. Gone without a trace, and with this motto: "My line will be that unformulated instruction which I have obeyed unknown to me, and which I will discover with surprise."

I n the fall of 1994, a Grès exhibition opened at the Costume Institute of the New York Metropolitan Museum of Art. Anne Grès wrote to *Women's Wear Daily*: "Thank you for your letter of September 22nd which I gave to my mother. Truly touched by the interest you show in her, she asked me to give you the answers to the questions you asked her."

Seeking to meet Madame Grès beginning in September 1994, I found myself ensnared in the net of a story with no name, where abolished time surrounds its prey, dead or alive, with delectation. I remember everything. The noise of the wine bottle that Anne Grès dropped in her kitchen as I was asking her questions about her mother. "Mother is gone. She doesn't know who I am anymore. She rests, she listens to music. It's as if a piece of her brain has been thrown into the garbage. I don't want anyone to see her. It would be like betraying her. She no longer wears her turban…" I remember the red puddle expanding on the floor, and the pieces of glass she swept up with a toy broom. I remember her son, with whom she lived in this house in the Var, along with her three dogs, Louloute, Clochard and Igor, her cat Ouistiti and her parrot. I remember the cold and the dust, those piles of objects and those chests that seemed to contain newspapers and treasures. There was key witness who gave me an appointment at the *Café de la Paix:* "You'll recognize me, I'll be wearing a turban." And I especially remember December 12th, 1994, at the town hall of the 17th arrondissement, where an employee held out that birth certificate, accompanied by a death certificate registered on November 24th, 1993.

madame Grès left us just as she had lived: very discreetly. History has labeled her the queen of drapery, a title she hated. "She was always able to take a fresh approach to the structures of clothing," remembers Peggy Huyn Kinh. Japanese couturiers from Rei Kawakubo to Junyo Watanabé could have identified with her book folds. "I'm not interested in old-fashioned styles, it's the future that excites me. I forget the past, I don't like old things, and I forget my collections once they're finished." With Madame Grès, a wimple could become a soft crepe collar, and a belt could become a free waist bracelet, through a "subtle match of the plumb-line, curves and oblique lines." Something ran through her, she was driven by a life force, just as her dresses came to life, like offerings for eternity. "Clothing follows the evolution of life, this is normal. But you have to keep a sense of shape and materials, you have to love beauty and the female body." For Madame Grès, seasons, countries and years gently rub shoulders. "The queen of the beach and the night," she was called by fashion columnist Pierre-Yves Guillen. Never has one celebrated with such subtlety the marriage of the chaste and the sensual, designing the apron of a real-fake boarding school girl in ebony-colored satin, to be worn naked. "Its beauty literally throws itself at you, and only the beautiful attracts the eye. The key is to have the eye able to appreciate it[12]."

Her layers are weightless: a long, negligently knotted skirt; billowed by the wind, a long split T-shirt becomes a "sun-top dress made of white wool jersey." From the height of her luxurious humility, a Bedouin coat held closed by a single button aristocratically descends the steps of the Paris Opera House. "With Alix, you notice a sensational evening coat in black and gold oilskin satin, creased in such a way that it looks like Cordovan leather," could be read in the September 1934 issue of Vogue. The art of illusion was her supreme luxury. "I always believed that life is an endless struggle, and I was convinced that if I abandoned that struggle, that life would abandon me." May these images be a tribute to her.

1. *Women's Wear Daily*, February 2, 1938.
2. Lucien François, *Comment un nom devient une griffe*, Gallimard, 1962.
3. *Alix Grès, L'Enigme d'un style*, L'Or des Iles, July 1992.
4. *Le Figaro littéraire*, February 5, 1968.
5. *Haute Couture, terre inconnue*, Hachette, 1956.
6. Lucien François, *op. cit.*
7. *Le Quotidien de Paris*, March 26, 1980.
8. *Lire*, May 1984.
9. *Lire*, May 1984.
10. *Libération*, July 28 and 29, 1984.
11. *Le Monde*, December 14, 1994.
12. *L'Art de Madame Grès*, Bunka Publishing Bureau, Bunka Shupan Kyoku, Japan, 1980.

Un nouveau
drapé prestigieux de Grès

Grès. Robe drapée en mousseline de Marcel Guillemin. Le tissu, blanc au corsage,
devient progressivement rose très pâle, puis rose soutenu. Gants de Hermès.

Grès. Les longs pans de jersey drapés
sur la poitrine donnent un effet de
taille haute. Jerseys de soie blanc
de Rémond, et mauve de Guillemin.

Le dos blousé

Grès. Redingote de lainage brun de Meyer. Le dos est très blousant, la taille pincée en paraît plus mince. Les emmanchures sont très larges.

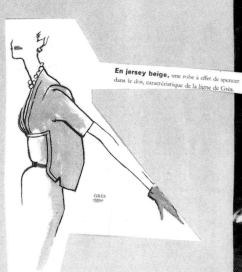

En jersey beige, une robe à effet de spencer dans le dos, caractéristique de la ligne de Grès.

GRÈS

GRÈS

David Weinerov

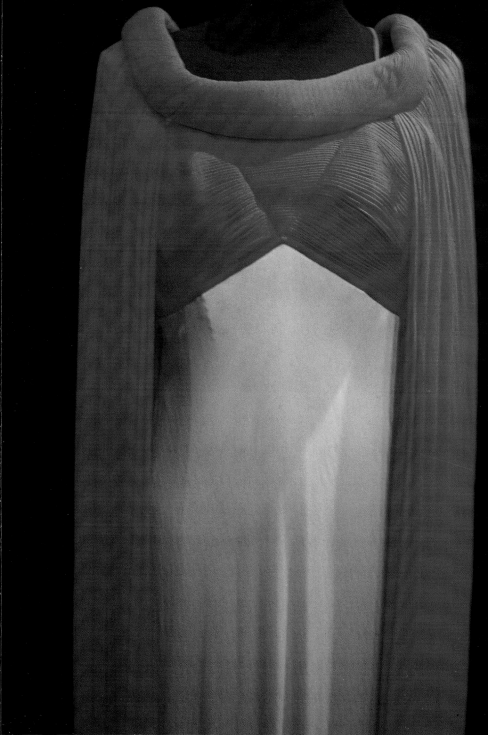

Chronology

1903: Germaine Emilie Krebs was born in Paris, in the 17th arrondissement, on November 30th.

1933: Her first identified model is a sports outfit, shown in June in *Vogue*.

1934: Hired by a fashion workshop located at 83, rue du Faubourg Saint-Honoré, as a dress designer. She quickly becomes the associate, under the name Alix. First successes with her Antiquity-style draped jerseys.

1935: First stage costumes for *La guerre de Troie n'aura pas lieu*, by Jean Giraudoux, directed by Louis Jouvet.

1939: Exhibits her works at the *Exposition Universelle* in Paris, and wins first prize for Haute Couture.

1941: *Alix*'s career ends due to a falling-out with her associates.

1942: Alone and without a sponsor, she creates a new second-floor company at 1, rue de la Paix, and names it "Grès," an anagram of the first name of her husband, Serge Czerefkov.

1943: Following her "blue white red" collection, her company is closed down. Madame Grès seeks refuge in the Pyrenees.

1945: The Grès company reopens.

1947: *She receives the French Legion of Honor.*

1958: She is the only French woman chosen by the Ford Foundation to help reorganize textile production in India.

1959: Launch of the perfume *Cabochard*.

1965: Launch of the perfume *Grès pour homme*.

1972: Madame Grès, the senior member of her profession, becomes President of the *Chambre Syndicale de la Couture* committee in Paris.

1976: She receives the *Dé d'or de la haute couture*, awarded for the first time. Launch of the perfume *Quiproquo*.

1978: On October 4th, Madame Grès receives the Creative leadership in the Art Professions Award in New York.

1981: Grès retrospective at the *Musée du Costume* in Paris.

1984: Sale of the company to Bernard Tapie.

The Théâtre de la mode *(1990). Evening gown: fitted bodice with long sleeves made of black silk book muslin, French pleats at waist, open ample skirt over green skirt; Caroline Reboux hat. © Photo: David Seidner.*

1986: Bernard Tapie sells the company to the Jacques Esterel group.
The Grès company is excluded from the Chambre Syndicale due to "failure to pay its dues."

1987: Liquidation of the company.

1988: The Japanese company Yagi Tsusho buys the couturier's name.
Last public appearance of Madame Grès at the Fashion Oscar ceremony at the Garnier Opera House, in Paris.

1990: Madame Grès leaves Paris with her daughter to live in a retirement home in the south of France.

1994: *Grès* retrospective organized by Richard Martin and Harold Koda, curators of the Costume Institute at the New York Metropolitan Museum of Art.
On December 14th, the daily *Le Monde* reveals the death of Madame Grès, which occurred on November 24th, 1993 and was not disclosed by her daughter in the name of a "love secret."

Grès

La guerre de Troie n'aura pas lieu, by Jean Giraudoux, with Louis Jouvet and
Madeline Ozeray (photo). Théâtre de l'Athénée, November 1935. Costumes
designed by Alix Grès. © Lipnitzki-Viollet.
Peach-colored silk jersey evening gown (1963). Metropolitan Museum of Art,
New York. © Sygma.

Black silk taffeta evening gown (1970). Metropolitan Museum of Art, New
York. © Sygma.
Bust of draped statue and Apollo's temple (1963), ancient Corinth. Photo:
Herbert List. © Max Scheler, The Herbert List Estate.

Drawing for Alix by Christian Bérard (1939). © ADAGP, Paris, 1999/Biblio-
thèque Forney, Paris.
Athens Acropolis: Erechtheus, column of north portico and northeast corner.
Photo: Herbert List. © Max Scheler, The Herbert List Estate.

Taya Thurman in a dress by Madame Grès (1980). © Photo: David Seidner.

Rough design of a dress by Grès (1939). Photo: Willy Maywald. © Association Willy Maywald/ADAGP, Paris, 1999.
"When I create a dress, I do it with the heart of a woman, and for the
woman who will wear it." © Photo: M. Desjardins/Rapho.

Press clippings from *Vogue* France, October 1952. © Courtesy of Jean-Michel
Chaufour.

Advertising design for Marcelle Alix. *Fémina*, 1946. © All rights reserved/ Bibliothèque Forney, Paris.
Brown double-skirt made of taffeta uni set over a grey silk jersey slip-on (1951). Weight, texture and color contrasts. Photo: Henry Clarke. © ADAGP, Paris, 1999/Bibliothèque Forney, Paris.

Models by Grès for the *Théâtre de la mode* exhibit held in Paris (1945), in sets made by Christian Bérard. Photo: Lido. © All rights reserved.
Madame Grès preparing the dolls for the *Théâtre de la mode.* Photo: Roger Schall. © Jean-Frédéric Schall/Musée de la Mode et du Textile collection, Paris.

Two dresses by Alix, worn by Lisa Fonssagrives. *Harper's Bazaar*, 1937. Photo: George Platt Lynes. © All rights reserved (left). © Photo: Eugène Rubin/ Archives Grès (right).

Evening outfit. Vest with peplum made of multicolor silk brocade (fabric created by Raoul Dufy, 1935). A similar model (with peplum) was created for Marlene Dietrich. Metropolitan Museum of Art, New York. © Sygma.
Evening gown by Alix (Spring 1938). Photo: Studio d'Ora. © All rights reserved.

Indian miniature, Pahari school, XVIIIth century, gouache on paper. © AKG Paris/ Jean-Louis Nou.
Model by Alix (Winter 1934). Photo: G. Saad. © All rights reserved.

Model by Alix, Pavillon de l'Elégance (1937). Photo: Wols. © All rights reserved.
Model by Grès (around 1960). © All rights reserved.

Madame Grès in 1946. © Photo: Eugène Rubin.
The sari was Alix's inspiration for this dress made of muslin embroidered with metal. Drawing: Eric (1935). © All rights reserved/Bibliothèque Forney, Paris.

Drawing by René Gruau for Alix (1937). © René Gruau/Archives Sylvie Nissen.
Silk jersey dress, photographed at the Louvre Museum, Paris (1948). © All rights reserved/Archives Grès.

Photo published in *Le Figaro Illustré,* September 1937. Photo: Joffé. © All rights reserved/Archives Grès.
Black taffeta evening gown by Grès (1950). Photo: Philippe Pottier. © All rights reserved/Musée de la Mode et du Textile collection, Paris.

Classic draped dress in white silk jersey, geranium-colored taffeta uni draping one shoulder and baring the other, and grey taffeta **uni full dress,** skirt gathered at waist, fitted corselet in white taffeta uni extending into a long court coat. Photo: Henry Clarke. © ADAGP, Paris, 1999/Bibliothèque Forney, Paris.

Grès press kit. Clippings from the *Officiel de la couture,* October 1953. © Courtesy Jean-Michel Chaufour.

Silk jersey dress. © Photo: Louis Faurer/Vogue France, March 1973/courtesy of Howard Greenberg Gallery, New York.
Rome, bas-relief: dancing maenad (end of IInd century). Museo dei conservatori, Rome. © All rights reserved.

Cabochard **perfume,** created in 1959. © Escada Parfum.
Madame Grès in her couture firm, located at 1, rue de la Paix, Paris (1950). © All rights reserved.

78

Black silk taffeta by Alix, opening down the back into a mauve, turquoise, pink and green pointe à godet. Solarized negative print, colorized during offset printing. Harper's Bazaar, February 1937. Photo: Man Ray. © Man Ray Trust/ADAGP, Paris, 1999.

Dress by Grès and *Cabochard* perfume (1959). © All rights reserved/Archives Grès.

Silk jersey strapless dress (1955). © Photo: Robert Doisneau/Rapho.

Two-color silk plisse crepe dress, top crossing over chest (1975). Christie's auction, September 17th, 1998. © Courtesy of Christie's, London.

Jackie Kennedy, dressed in a Grès dress, and Robert Frost, during the reception given at the White House in honor of the Nobel prize winners (1962). Jackie and John Fitzgerald Kennedy during that same reception. Photos: Arthur Rickerby. © Life Magazine/PPCM.

Twiggy in Grès dress (March 1967). Photo: Bert Stern, courtesy of Vogue. © 1967 (renewed 1995) by The Condé Nast Publication, Inc.

Nathalie, model in Grès coat (Kairouan, 1950). Photo: Louise Dahl-Wolfe. © Staley-Wise Gallery/Musée de la Mode et du Textile collection, Paris.

Draped dress fitted at waist with belt. Vogue US, 1965. © Photo: William Klein.

Long evening gown in ivory- and coral-colored silk jersey, coral-colored cape (late 1950's). Christie's auction, September 17th, 1998. © Courtesy of Christie's, London.

Models by Grès, exhibited in the Noailles villa (Hyères, Summer 1992). Private collection. © Photos: Guy and Richard Barsotti.

Théâtre de la mode, version 1990. Model by Grès: dress coat in rust-colored silk velvet, fan-shaped draped bodice, puffed sleeves fitted at elbows; Caroline Reboux hat. © Photo: David Seidner.

Deborah Klein wearing a Grès dress (1986). © Photo: David Seidner.

The author wishes to thank Marc Audibert, Jacques Biob and Delphine Priollaud for their precious help.

The publisher would like to thank the Grès Company for their help in preparing this book. Also thanks to Richard and Guy Barsotti, Louis Faurer, William Klein, Jean-Louis Nou, Eugène Rubin, David Seidner and Bert Stern. Lastly, this book could not have been made without the kind contributions of David Abel (*Vogue* US), Nicole Chamson (ADAGP, Paris), Jean-Michel Chaufour, Francine Deroudile (Rapho), Margit Erb (Howard Greenberg Gallery), the Bibliothèque Forney, Thierry Freiberg (Sygma), Anne Herme (Roger-Viollet), Hervé (AKG), Elsa Joly Malhomme (Christie's, Paris), Noémie Mainguet, Matthew Marden (Staley-Wise Gallery), Florence Marty (Escada), Emmanuelle Montet and Marie-Hélène Poix (Musée de la Mode et du Textile, Paris), Franck Munoz (Télimage), Madame Nieman (association Willy Maywald), Pierre-Louis (William Klein), Jean-Frédéric Schall, Valérie and Jean-Christophe (PPCM), Olivier Rometti, Max Scheler (The Herbert List Estate), Suzette Shield's and Susy Mayor (Christie's, London), Véronique (Magnum), and Michèle Zauquin (*Vogue* France).